This book is dedicated to
our beautiful granddaughter Mitike.

©2011 by the author of this book.
The book author retains sole copyright
to his or her contributions to this book.

ETHIOPIAN COOKBOOK

Rachel Pambrun　　　Linda Johnson　　　Carole Bolick

AUTHOR
Rachel Pambrun

COOKS
Linda Johnson
Carole Bolick

PHOTO EDITOR
Britta Kokemor Quinlan

ETHIOPIAN COOKBOOK

I am a little pencil in the hand of a writing God who is sending a love letter to the world
- Mother Teresa

The world is facing a hunger crisis unlike anything it has seen in more than 50 years.
Every day, almost 16,000 children die from hunger-related causes. That's one child every five seconds.
In 2010, 7.6 million children died worldwide before their 5th birthday.
These communities need access to safe water, agricultural supplies and training,
education, basic medical attention and small business opportunities.
Together we can help.

Proceeds from the sale of this book will help bring about change for suffering African communities.
In this book we share the unique traditions and flavours of Ethiopian Cuisine,
in support of millions of Africans in need.

Our deepest gratitude to all who contributed their time and creativity to the making of this book.

Every action in our lives touches on some chord that will vibrate in eternity
- Edwin Hubbel Chapin

ETHIOPIA

Ethiopia is a place of high plateaus and low-lying plains.
This ancient country is called the land of thirteen months of sunshine, as the Ethiopian calendar has twelve months of thirty days, and an extra month of five days called Pagume.
The climate is balmy and pleasant with rain falling rarely except in the summer months.

Primitive and modern cultures exist side by side in Ethiopia.
In the villages, families live in Tukels made of stone with thatched roofs, and life goes on today much as it has for centuries.
In Addis Ababa, there are new white buildings of reinforced concrete in the midst of bustling, energetic people.
Women with exquisite facial bone structure wear Shamas, a gauzelike white fabric covering them from head to foot.
Men wear either Ethiopian robes or Western attire.

The open-air market of Addis, Ethiopia is the largest and most exciting in all of Africa.
The market seems to stretch for miles.
Everything is on display, from clothing and household wares to treadle sewing machines. For the food at these markets, women sit cross-legged on the ground with tiny scales to measure spices for the Wat. Grains, called Tef, in huge bags are ready for the housewives who make Injera bread.
The low stands are heaped with citrus fruits, bananas, grapes, pomegranates, figs, custard apples which are a delectable tropical fruit, as well as vegetables of all kinds, including the wonderful red onion of this area.
The meats on sale are beef, lamb, and goat. You'll find lab, the soft cheese wrapped and kept cool in banana leaves.

ETHIOPIAN CUISINE

Ethiopian food is a spicy mix of vegetable and lentil stews and slow-simmered meats.
The hottest, most peppery food in all of Africa is found in Ethiopia.
While most Ethiopian cuisine is indigenous, over time ingredients such as red chillies, ginger, and spices have enriched its flavours.
Grains like millet, sorghum, wheat and ancient Teff form the basic breadstuffs of the diet.

Essential components of Ethiopian cooking are Injera bread, Berbere, a red pepper spice
and Niter Kibbeh, a spice-infused clarified butter.
Most foods have a stewy consistency. Alichas are mild stews. Wats are stews with the spicy flavour of Berbere.
Desserts are not really served in Ethiopia, but Iab, similar to a mixture of cottage cheese and yogurt,
is traditionally the final course of a meal.

Dietary restrictions in religions have given rise to a wide variety of both meat and vegetarian dishes.
There are fast days when meat is prohibited and lentils, peas, and chick peas are used in making the Wat and Alicha.
No one is permitted to eat pork.

Most farming in Ethiopia is subsistence, so the vegetables and animals are often grown and raised at home.
Ethiopia has been called the "Land of Bread and Honey".
The ancient practice of beekeeping produces exquisite honey.
Honey is fermented to Tej, a honey wine.

SERVING DINNER IN ETHIOPIA

A meal in Ethiopia is an experience!
The guests are seated round the table on stools about eight inches high and a Mesab, a handmade wicker hourglass-shaped table and a designed domed cover is set before them.

A tall, stunning woman with characteristically high cheekbones and soft skin, dressed in a Shama, carries a long-spouted copper pitcher in her right hand, a copper basin in her left hand, and a towel over her left arm.
She pours warm water over the fingers of your right hand, holding the basin to catch the excess, and you wipe your hands on the towel that hangs over her arm.

The meal is then served on a large platter that is draped with crepe-like Injera bread.
All guests eat from this one platter.
Various dishes are brought to the table in enamel bowls and portioned out onto the Injera.
Guests simply tear off a piece of the bread, use it to scoop up some of the various stews and pop it in their mouths.

The server then returns with individual long-necked bottles from which you drink Tej, an amber-coloured honey wine which is put on a little table close by.
She may also serve beverages such as weakly carbonated water or Telba, a flaxseed drink.
Another hand washing ends the meal and strong coffee is served on a tray in tiny Japanese cups served black with sugar.
Frankincense is then burned.

STAPLE ITEMS

Two essential components of Ethiopian cooking are Berbere, peppery spice,
and Niter Kibbeh, spiced clarified butter.
Berbere, along with Niter Kibbeh, supplies one of the unique flavours of Ethiopian cuisine.
These two items are frequently used and are the perfect place to begin your Ethiopian Cooking.

Essential spices in Ethiopian cooking are; fenugreek seeds, crushed mustard seeds, crushed caraway seeds,
cardamom seeds, cardamom pods, whole cumin, whole peppercorns, whole cloves,
allspice berries, dried chillies, red pepper flakes,
paprika, salt, pepper, turmeric, cayenne pepper,
nutmeg, cinnamon,
gingerroot, ground ginger, crushed garlic,
basil, oregano, parsley and coriander.

The most commonly used vegetables are; onions, carrots, green peas, lentils, tomatoes, potatoes,
lemons, cabbage, sweet potatoes, cucumbers and corn.

Important cooking utensils are; spice grinder, large cast iron skillet, frying pan, food processor or blender and if possible an Injera platter.

INDEX

Staple Items
Red Pepper Spice.................................. 1
Spiced Clarified Butter....................... 2

Wat Spicy Stews Served with Injera or Kita
Onion... 3
Vegetable... 4
Chickpea.. 5
Lentil... 6
Chicken / Zucchini / Lamb................. 7

Alicha Mild Stews Served with Injera or Kita
Vegetable... 8
Chicken.. 9
Beef / Lamb....................................... 10

Meals Served with Rice or Kita
Vegetable Stew................................. 11
Beef Stew.. 12
Sautéed Lamb................................... 13
Lamb.. 14
Mashed Potatoes.............................. 15
Hot and Spicy African Wraps............ 16

Breads
Flatbread... 17
Unleavened Flatbread...................... 18
Spiced Honey Bread......................... 19

Before and After Dinner Foods
Fried Turnover................................... 20
Lentil Soup.. 21
Spicy Lentil Salad.............................. 22
Tomato and Cucumber Salad........... 23
Hot Cabbage Salad........................... 24
Little Fried Snacks............................ 25
Fresh Cheese.................................... 26

Beverages
Flaxseed Beverage........................... 27
Honey Wine....................................... 28

ETHIOPIAN COOKBOOK

Red Pepper Spice
Berbere

Description: *Berbere* is a red pepper spice mixture and a key ingredient in Ethiopian cuisine.

Preparation Time: 5 minutes
Cooking Time: 2 minutes

Serving Size: 1/3 cup

Ingredients:

Whole cumin	2 tsp
Red pepper flakes	1 tsp
Cardamom seeds	1 tsp
Fenugreek seeds	1 tsp
Whole peppercorns	8
Allspice berries	6
Whole cloves	4
Paprika	1 tbsp
Salt	1 tbsp
Ground ginger	1 tsp
Turmeric	1 tsp
Cayenne pepper	1 tsp
Nutmeg	1/2 tsp

Method:
1. Heat a cast-iron skillet over medium flame. Add the whole spices and toast, stirring for 2 to 3 minutes until they give off their aroma. Do not burn. Remove from heat.
2. Put the spices into a spice or coffee grinder and grind to a powder.

For Variation:
1. You can make Berbere as spicy or as mild as you like by varying the amount of pepper flakes and cayenne pepper.

ETHIOPIAN COOKBOOK

Spiced Clarified Butter
Niter Kibbeh

Description: *Niter kibbeh* is a spiced, clarified butter and a very important cooking medium in Ethiopian cuisine. It adds an incomparable flavour to dishes. Plain butter or oil can be substituted in Ethiopian recipes if you don't have the time to make *niter kibbeh*, but something special will be missing.

Preparation Time: 5 minutes
Cooking Time: 1 hour

Serving Size: 2 cups

Ingredients:

Unsalted butter	1 lb
Onion (chopped)	1 cup
Garlic (crushed)	2-3 cloves
Gingerroot (cut in ¼ inch slices)	2-3 pieces
Cardamom pods	3-4
Ground cinnamon	1 tsp
Whole cloves	3-4
Fenugreek seeds	1 tsp
Turmeric	1/2 tsp

Method:

1. Place the butter in a small saucepan and melt over low heat.
2. Add the remaining ingredients and simmer on the lowest possible heat for about 1 hour.
3. Pour the clear golden liquid off the top leaving all the solids in the bottom of the pan. Strain if necessary. Discard solids.
4. Store in the refrigerator or freezer and use as needed.

ETHIOPIAN COOKBOOK

WAT

Wats are thick, spicy stews that are served on top of Injera bread.
Ethiopians eat with their right hands,
using pieces of Injera to pick up bites of Wat entrees.
Utensils are rarely used with this dish.

ETHIOPIAN COOKBOOK

Onion Wat
Sum Sikil

Preparation Time: 20 minutes
Cooking Time: 30 minutes

Serving Size: 6

Ingredients:

Red onions (chopped)	6 cups
Garlic (chopped)	3 tbsp
Olive oil	1 cup
Green chilli paste	1 tbsp
Salt	1 tbsp
Curry powder	1 tbsp
Ground cardamom	1 tbsp
Ground cloves	1 tsp
Oregano	1 tsp
Sweet basil	1 tsp
Ground cinnamon	1 tsp
Tomato paste	1 ½ cups

Method:
1. Chop onions and garlic. Put them into a covered casserole dish, without oil or water. At high heat, stir constantly until the onions appear cooked.
2. Add one cup of olive oil. Lower heat to medium, and simmer uncovered for 10 minutes.
3. Add green chilli paste and stir until completely blended.
4. Stirring all the while, add salt, curry powder, ground cardamom, ground cloves, oregano, sweet basil and ground cinnamon.
5. Reduce heat to low and simmer 10 minutes.
6. If desired, add tomato paste and stir until completely blended.
7. Simmer for an additional 10 minutes.

Vegetable Wat
Yatakelt

Preparation Time: 5 minutes
Cooking Time: 30 minutes

Serving Size: 6

Ingredients:

Ingredient	Amount
Red onions (finely chopped)	1 cup
Garlic (minced)	2 cloves
Berbere	1 tsp
Paprika	1 tsp
Niter kibbeh	1/4 cup
Green beans (cut in thirds)	1 cup
Carrots (chopped)	1 cup
Potatoes (cubed)	1 cup
Tomatoes (chopped)	1 cup
Tomato paste	¼ cup
Vegetable stock	2 cups
Salt	to taste
Black pepper	to taste
Fresh parsley (chopped)	1/4 cup
Injera	2 batches
Plain yogurt or cottage cheese	

Method:

1. Sauté the onions, garlic, berbere and paprika in the niter kibbeh for 2 minutes.
2. Add the beans, carrots, and potatoes. Continue to sauté for 10 minutes, stirring occasionally to prevent burning.
3. Add the chopped tomatoes, tomato paste and the vegetable stock.
4. Bring to a boil and then simmer for 15 minutes, or until all of the vegetables are tender.
5. Add salt and pepper to taste and mix in the parsley.
6. Serve with Injera and yogurt or cottage cheese.

ETHIOPIAN COOKBOOK

Chickpea Wat
Yeshiro

Preparation Time: 15 minutes
Cooking Time: 45 minutes

Serving Size: 6

Ingredients:

Olive oil	2 tbsp
Red onion (finely chopped)	1
Carrots (finely chopped)	2
Potato (peeled, chopped)	1
Cayenne pepper	1/2 tsp
Paprika	1/2 tsp
Ground ginger	1/2 tsp
Salt	1/2 tsp
Black pepper	1/2 tsp
Cumin	1/4 tsp
Cardamom	1/4 tsp
Tomato paste	1 tbsp
Chickpeas (drained, rinsed)	1 cup
Water	1 ½ cups
Peas	1 cup

Method:

1. Heat the oil in a large pot over medium heat. Add the onion, cover and cook for 5 minutes until softened.
2. Add the carrots and potato, cover and cook 10 minutes longer.
3. Remove and cover and stir in cayenne, paprika, ginger, salt, pepper, cumin, cardamom and tomato paste.
4. Add chickpeas and water and bring to a boil. Reduce heat to low and simmer for 20 minutes, covered.
5. Stir in green peas and taste to adjust seasonings. Simmer for 10 more minutes until vegetables are tender and the flavour is developed. Add a bit more water if needed.

ETHIOPIAN COOKBOOK

Lentil Wat
Yemesir

Preparation Time: 5 minutes
Cooking Time: 1 hour

Serving Size: 4 to 6

Ingredients:

Onions (chopped)	2 cups
Garlic (crushed)	2 cloves
Ginger (peeled, minced)	2 tsp
Oil, butter or niter kibbeh	1/4 cup
Turmeric	1 tsp
Paprika	2 tbsp
Cayenne pepper	1/2 to 2 tsp
Red lentils (rinsed)	2 cups
Water or stock	4 cups
Salt	to taste
Black pepper	to taste

Method:
1. Place the onion, garlic and ginger in a food processor or blender and puree. Add a little water if necessary.
2. Heat the oil, butter or niter kibbeh in a large, heavy-bottomed saucepan over medium heat.
3. Add turmeric, paprika and cayenne pepper. Stir rapidly for 30 seconds to color the oil and cook spices through.
4. Add the onion puree and sauté for 5 to 20 minutes, until the excess moisture evaporates and the onion loses its raw aroma.
5. Add lentils and water to the saucepan. Bring to a boil, reduce heat to low, and simmer for 30 to 40 minutes until lentils are cooked through and fall apart. Add water if necessary to keep the lentils from drying out.
6. Stir in salt and pepper to taste.

For Variation:
1. To make *Shiro Wat*; use split green peas instead of lentils.
2. Substitute yellow lentils if you prefer.

Chicken, Zucchini or Lamb Wat
Doro, Sik Sik, Sega

Preparation Time: 40 minutes
Cooking Time: 45 minutes

Serving Size: 4 to 6

Ingredients:

Skinless chicken legs and thighs	2 lbs
Lemon (juice)	1
Salt	2 tsp
Onions (chopped)	2
Garlic (crushed)	2 tbsp
Gingerroot (peeled, chopped)	1 tbsp
Oil, butter or niter kibbeh	1/4 cup
Paprika	2 tbsp
Berbere	2 tsp
Water or stock	3/4 cup
Red wine	1/3 cup
Cayenne pepper	from 1 tsp
Salt	to taste
Black pepper	to taste
Hard boiled eggs	4

Method:

1. Mix together the chicken pieces, lemon juice and salt in a large, non-reactive bowl and set aside to marinate for 30 minutes.
2. While the chicken is marinating, puree the onions, garlic and ginger in a food processor or blender. Add a little water if necessary.
3. Heat the oil, butter or niter kibbeh in a large pot over medium flame. Add the paprika and stir for 1 minute to color the oil and cook the spice through. Do not burn. Stir in the berbere paste and cook for another 2 to 3 minutes.
4. Add the onion-garlic-ginger puree and sauté for 5 to 10 minutes until most of the moisture evaporates and the onion cooks down and loses its raw aroma. Do not allow the mixture to burn.
5. Pour in the water or stock and wine. Stir in the chicken pieces (without the marinade), cayenne, salt and pepper to taste. Bring to a boil, reduce heat to low, cover and simmer for 45 minutes. Add water as necessary to maintain a sauce-like consistency.
6. Add the whole hard boiled eggs and continue to cook for another 10 to 15 minutes, or until the chicken is cooked through and very tender.
7. Adjust seasoning and serve hot with Injera or rice.

ETHIOPIAN COOKBOOK

For Variation:
1. *Chicken Wat* is traditionally very spicy, but you can adjust the amount of cayenne pepper to your liking.

2. To make *Sik Sik Wat,* substitute 2 lbs of small zucchini, halved and quartered. Proceed with the recipe, but just cook long enough for the zucchini to be cooked through and soft.

3. To make *Sega Wat*, substitute 2 lbs of lamb for the chicken in this recipe.

ETHIOPIAN COOKBOOK

ALICHA

Alichas are mild but tasteful stews that are served on top of Injera bread. Alicha is mildly spiced Ethiopian stew because berbere, the spicy Ethiopian paste, is not added to the pot.

ETHIOPIAN COOKBOOK

Vegetable Alicha
Yatakelt

Preparation Time: 10 minutes
Cooking Time: 25 minutes

Serving Size: 6 to 8

Ingredients:

Red onions	1 cup
Oil	4 tbsp
Carrots (cut in 1 inch slices)	4
Green peppers (cut in quarters)	4
Water	3 cups
Tomato paste	1/2 cup
Salt	2 tsp
Ground ginger	1/2 tsp
Potatoes (cut in thick slices)	4
Tomatoes	2
Cabbage wedges (cut in 1 inch cubes)	8
Salt	to taste
Black pepper	to taste

Method:

1. In a 4-quart saucepan, sauté onions in oil until soft but not brown.
2. Add carrots, green peppers, water, tomato paste, salt and ground ginger.
3. Cook for 10 minutes covered. Add potatoes.
4. Plunge tomatoes in boiling water and remove skins. Cut in 8 wedges each and add to stew.
5. Cover and cook for 10 minutes.
6. Add cabbage wedges.
7. Sprinkle with salt and pepper.
8. Cook until vegetables are tender.
9. Correct the seasoning.

ETHIOPIAN COOKBOOK

Chicken Alicha
Doro

Preparation Time: 10 minutes
Cooking Time: 55 minutes

Serving Size: 4

Ingredients:

Chicken (cut in parts, without skin)	1 lb
Lime (juice)	1
Red onions	6 cups
Niter kibbeh	2 cups
Red wine	1/2 cup
Black pepper	1/4 tsp
Garlic powder	1/4 tsp
Ground ginger	1/4 tsp
Salt	to taste
Water	4 cups
Hard-boiled eggs	4

Method:
1. Wash the chicken parts and soak in water with lime juice.
2. In a large pot, fry the onions until tender. Add niter kibbeh and stir. Add ½ cup of water and the wine. Add spices.
3. Add the chicken.
4. Add more water if necessary, and cook for 45 minutes until the sauce is reduced.
5. Add eggs (if desired) and serve.

ETHIOPIAN COOKBOOK

Beef or Lamb Alicha
Saga, Sega

Preparation Time: 15 minutes
Cooking Time: 1 hour

Serving Size: 6

Ingredients:

Red onion (sliced)	1 cup
Corn oil	2 tbsp
Beef or lamb	2 lbs
Garlic cloves (sliced)	2
Salt	1 tsp
Hot green chilli pepper (sliced)	1
Gingerroot (crushed)	1/4 tsp
Mustard seeds (crushed)	1/4 tsp
Caraway seed (crushed)	1/4 tsp
Ground turmeric	1/4 tsp
Water	1/2 cups

Method:

1. In dry pan over medium heat, stir-fry onions for 2 minutes.
2. Add the oil and stir-fry 1 minute longer. Add the meat and brown 5 minutes, stirring frequently.
3. Add all of the spices and seasonings at one time and stir well.
4. Add the water and bring to a boil. Cover the pan and cook over low heat for 45 minutes, or until the meat is tender.
5. Should the curry dry out too quickly, add another ½ cup water.
6. At the end of the 45 minutes, there should be very little sauce.
7. Serve warm or at room temperature.

ETHIOPIAN COOKBOOK

MEALS SERVED WITH RICE OR KITA

Ethiopian meals offer taste filled enjoyment.
These meals are a mix of spicy and mild dishes rich in flavour.

Vegetable Stew
Yetakelt

Preparation Time: 15 minutes
Cooking Time: 40 minutes

Serving Size: 4 to 6

Ingredients:

Ingredient	Amount
Oil	4 tbsp
Onions (chopped)	1 cup
Berbere	3 tsp
Carrots (cut in 1 inch slices)	3
Green bell peppers (quartered)	3
Water	3 cups
Tomato sauce	3/4 cups
Salt	2 tsp
Ground ginger	1/2 tsp
Potatoes (cut in thick slices)	4
Tomatoes (skinned, cut in wedges)	2
Cabbage (cut in 1 inch wedges)	8
Black pepper	to taste

Method:

1. Add the oil and onions to a large saucepan and fry on medium for 5 minutes or until the onions have softened.
2. Add berbere and fry for one minute.
3. Add carrots, green peppers, water, tomato sauce, salt and ground ginger. Bring to a simmer and cook for 10 minutes.
4. Add potatoes and tomatoes. Cover and cook for 10 minutes.
5. Add cabbage. Season to taste and cook for 25 minutes or until the vegetables are completely tender.

Beef Stew
Saga

Preparation Time: 30 minutes
Cooking Time: 1 hour

Serving Size: 8

Ingredients:

Butter or niter kibbeh	½ cup
Red onions (chopped finely)	3
Chilli paste	1/4 cup
Canned crushed tomatoes	1 cup
Beef brisket (cut in 1/2 inch cubes)	2 lbs

Method:

1. Heat a pan (3 to 4 inches deep).
2. Add half of the butter or niter kibbeh.
3. Once butter is melted, add the onions and cook it until the onions are caramelized.
4. Add chilli paste to the cooked onions. Cook for 15 minutes, stirring often and adding a drop of water as needed to prevent it from drying out.
5. Add tomatoes and cook for 30 minutes more, stirring it often and adding a drop of water as needed to prevent it from drying out.
6. Add beef to the cooking paste and cook covered for 25 minutes or until cooked fully.

Sautéed Lamb or Beef
Gomen Sega

Preparation Time: 5 minutes
Cooking Time: 15 minutes

Serving Size: 4 to 6

Ingredients:

Lean lamb or beef (cut in long strips)	1 lb
Garlic clove	1
Olive oil	1 tbsp
Sweet onion (thinly sliced)	1
Green hot peppers (thinly sliced)	3
Red bell pepper (thinly sliced)	1
Salt	a pinch
Butter	1 tbsp
Berbere spice	3-4 tbsp

Method:
1. Mix meat with garlic.
2. Heat oil over medium-high heat.
3. Saute onion and hot peppers for 5 minutes, or until onion is light golden.
5. Add red bell pepper and salt. Sauté 2 to 3 minutes until red pepper is tender.
6. Transfer onion mixture to a bowl.
7. In same pan, melt butter over high heat and sauté meat mixture for 2 minutes.
8. Stir in berbere spice mix to taste. Sauté for 30 seconds.
9. Serve with Injera or Tomato and Cucumber salad.

ETHIOPIAN COOKBOOK

Lamb
Sega

Preparation Time: 10 minutes
Cooking Time: 1 hour

Serving Size: 6

Ingredients:

Mustard greens (chopped)	4 lbs
Beef (diced)	2 lbs
Red onion (chopped)	1
Medium green pepper (chopped)	2
Salt	to taste
Black pepper	to taste
Niter kibbeh	6 tbsp
Medium scallion (chopped)	8
Medium serrano pepper (chopped)	4

Method:
1. Place mustard greens in a large pot and simmer for 10 minutes. Do not add water. Enough water clings to the greens in the cleaning process.
2. Drain and set aside.
3. In Dutch oven, sauté beef, onion, green pepper, salt and pepper until beef is brown.
4. Add mustard greens and remaining ingredients.
5. Cook for 1 hour or until liquid in pan has evaporated.

ETHIOPIAN COOKBOOK

Mashed Potatoes
Solanum Tubersum

Preparation Time: 15 minutes
Cooking Time: 25 minutes

Serving Size: 6

Ingredients:

Potatoes (diced)	2 ¼ cups
Sweet potatoes (diced)	1 ¾ cups
Whole kernel corn	1 cup
Light coconut milk	3/4 cup
Olive oil	1 tbsp
Butter	1 tbsp
Curry powder	1 tsp
Salt	1/2 tsp
Turmeric	1/4 tsp

Method:
1. Place potatoes and sweet potatoes in a saucepan. Cover with water and bring to a boil.
2. Reduce heat and simmer for 10 minutes, or until potatoes are almost tender.
3. Add corn to pan and cook 5 minutes, or until potatoes are tender.
4. Drain well. Place potato mixture in a large bowl, and mash potato mixture with a potato masher.
5. Combine coconut milk, oil, and butter in a small saucepan. Bring to a boil.
6. Stir milk mixture, curry, salt and turmeric into potato mixture.

ETHIOPIAN COOKBOOK

Hot and Spicy African Wraps
Doro

Preparation Time: 30 minutes
Cooking Time: 3 hours and 20 minutes

Serving Size: 4

Ingredients:

Chicken thigh fillet	2 lbs
Lemon (juice)	1
Salt	1/2 tbsp
Onion	1
Garlic cloves	2
Olive oil	1 tbsp
Berbere	2 tsp
Ginger (minced)	1 tbsp
Nutmeg	a pinch
Ground cardamom	a pinch
Red wine	1/4 cup
Chicken stock	2 cups
Tomato paste	1/2 cup
Coriander (chopped)	1 cup
Kita	4
Butter	2 tbsp

Method:
1. Place chicken in dish and cover with lemon juice and salt. Marinate in fridge for 30 minutes.
2. Chop onion and garlic. Cook in a large heavy pot with the olive oil until soft.
3. Add berbere mix, ginger, nutmeg, cardamom and stir-fry for 1 minute.
4. Add wine, stock and tomato paste and bring to simmer.
5. Add chicken and marinade mixture. Bring to boil, then reduce to simmer.
6. Simmer at very low temperature with lid on for 3 hours, stirring frequently and ensuring stew doesn't dry out or stick to bottom.
7. Add coriander.
8. Melt butter in frying pan. Cook Kita quickly turning so they puff up.
9. Fill Kita with stew and wrap.

BREADS

Injera is a yeast-risen flatbread with a unique, slightly spongy texture. Traditionally made out of teff flour, it is a national dish in Ethiopia served with Wats and Alichas.

Kita is unleavened flat bread with no yeast or baking powder and a staple food among the people of Africa.

Spiced Honey Bread is a tender, lightly sweet loaf that makes good use of Ethiopia's abundant honey.

Flatbread

Injera

Preparation Time: 5 minutes
Cooking Time: 25 minutes

Serving Size: 6 to 8 Crepes

Ingredients:

Teff Flour	1 ½ cups
Water	2 cups
Salt	1/2 tsp
Vegetable oil	
Lemon (juice)	1

Method:

1. Mix the teff flour with the water. Cover with a towel and let stand at room temperature until it bubbles and has fermented. The consistency should be comparable to a very thin pancake batter. This process may take up to 3 days. Each morning, gently disturb the mixture with a wooden spoon. There should be bubbles forming on the surface, it should smell sour and water should have risen to the top. If not yet ready, cover again and let stand again overnight.
2. Gradually stir in the salt until well mixed.
3. Preheat a large cast-iron skillet over a medium heat.
4. Wipe the skillet with a little oil using a paper towel.
5. Ladle about 1/2 cup of batter to cover the bottom of the skillet. Spread the batter around immediately with a spatula to make a large crepe.
6. Let bake in the skillet about 2 to 3 minutes, until holes form in the Injera and the edges begin to dry out.
7. Carefully turn the Injera over and cook on second side for 1 to 2 minutes. Try to not brown too much. Remove the Injera to a platter to cool.
8. Repeat with the rest of the batter, wiping the skillet clean with an oiled paper towel each time. Place plastic or foil between Injera so that they do not stick.
9. After the batter is used up, brush each Injera with the lemon juice.
10. Serve immediately or keep covered in a warm oven.

ETHIOPIAN COOKBOOK

Unleavened Flatbread
Kita

Preparation Time: 7 minutes
Cooking Time: 10 minutes

Serving Size: 12 to 14 Crepes

Ingredients:

All purpose flour	1 cup
Whole wheat flour	1 cup
Oil	1/2 cup
Salt	1 tsp
Water	1 cup

Method:
1. Heat oil in cast-iron skillet.
2. Mix flours and salt together in a bowl and salt. Gradually add the heated oil.
3. Gradually add up to 1 cup of lukewarm water while kneading to make dough.
4. Spread flour on a flat clean surface and form bun sized dough.
5. Roll out the dough with a rolling pin on the floured board until very thin and roughly in a round shape.
6. Cook in the cast-iron skillet until slightly puffed and brown.

Variations:
1. You can deep fry the Kita in oil if you would like to have them puff up.
2. Depending on what you are serving, you can spice with sage, thyme and summer savoury.

Spiced Honey Bread
Yemarin Yewotet Dabo

Preparation Time: 2 hours
Cooking Time: 1 hour

Serving Size: 1 loaf

Ingredients:

Active dry yeast	1/4 oz
Lukewarm water	1/4 cup
Egg (beaten)	1
Honey	1/2 cup
Ground coriander	1 tbsp
Ground cinnamon	1 tsp
Ground cloves	1/2 tsp
Salt	1 tsp
Warm milk	1 cup
Butter (melted)	6 tbsp
Flour	4-5 cups

Method:
1. Preheat oven to 325°F.
2. In a small bowl, stir together the yeast and 1/4 cup warm water. Set for about 10 minutes.
3. In a large bowl, beat together the egg, honey, spices and salt until smooth. Stir in the milk and melted butter.
4. Stir in the flour, 1/2 cup at a time, mixing to form a soft, smooth dough. Do not add all of the flour if the dough gets too stiff. Add more flour if the dough gets too sticky.
5. Remove the dough to a lightly floured work surface and knead for 10 minutes to form a smooth, elastic dough.
6. Place the dough in a large, lightly oiled bowl, cover with plastic wrap and let rise in a warm place until doubled in size, about 1 ½ hours.
7. Remove the dough again to a lightly floured work surface and punch down the dough. Knead for 1 minute. Form the dough into a round and place on an oiled baking sheet. Allow to rise again another 30 to 45 minutes.
8. Place bread on baking sheet in the oven and bake 45 minutes to 1 hour until bread is lightly browned and sounds hollow.

ETHIOPIAN COOKBOOK

BEFORE AND AFTER DINNER FOODS
Rich, spicy and complex Ethiopian flavours wake up the senses in these wonderful dishes.

Fried Turnover
Sambusa

Preparation Time: 20 minutes
Cooking Time: 30 minutes

Serving Size: 48

Ingredients:

Red onion (finely chopped)	1/2 cup
Lean ground lamb or beef (browned)	1 lb
Ginger (minced)	1/2 tsp
Ground turmeric	1/2 tsp
Garlic (minced)	1/2 tsp
Cayenne pepper	1/2 tsp
Salt	to taste
Cinnamon	1/2 tsp
Coriander sprigs (chopped)	4
Mint sprigs (chopped)	3
Water	2 cups
Wonton wrappers	48

Method:

1. Combine all ingredients (except for wonton wrappers) in a heavy saucepan.
2. Bring to a boil and stir to keep smooth.
3. Reduce heat to medium and let mixture simmer uncovered.
4. Correct flavour for spices and salt.
5. As water simmers away, stir often to prevent mixture from sticking, especially during final stages.
6. Cook until all liquid evaporates.
7. If ground meat has a lot of fat, drain off at this point.
8. Let mixture cool slightly before stuffing.
9. Fill wonton wrappers with 1 to 2 tsp of filling. Moisten and press the edges together in a triangle shape.
10. Fry the Sambusas, several at a time, until golden brown on both sides. Place the golden brown Sambusas on paper towel to rid of excess oil.
11. Serve hot or cold and with or without chutney.

Lentil Soup
Yemiser

Preparation Time: 10 minutes
Cooking Time: 20 minutes

Serving Size: 8

Ingredients:

Dried brown or rinsed canned lentils	1 cup
Onion (finely chopped)	1 cup
Garlic (minced)	2 cloves
Niter kibbeh	1/4 cup
Berbere	1 tsp
Ground cumin seeds	1 tsp
Paprika	1 tsp
Tomato (finely chopped)	2 cups
Tomato paste	1/2 cup
Vegetable stock or water	1 cup
Green peas	1 cup
Salt	to taste
Black pepper	to taste

Method:

1. Rinse and cook the lentils.
2. Meanwhile sauté the onions and garlic in the niter kibbeh until the onions are translucent.
3. Add the berbere, cumin and paprika. Sauté for a few minutes more, stirring occasionally to prevent burning.
4. Mix in the chopped tomatoes and tomato paste. Simmer for another 5 to 10 minutes.
5. Add vegetable stock or water and continue simmering.
6. When the lentils are cooked, drain and mix them into the sauté mixture.
7. Add the green peas and cook for another 5 minutes. Add salt and pepper to taste.

Spicy Lentil Salad
Azifa

Preparation Time: 10 minutes
Cooking Time: 30 minutes

Serving Size: 4

Ingredients:

Lentils	1/2 lb
Garlic (crushed)	1/4 tsp
Red onion	1/2 cup
Canned green chillies (chopped)	1/4 cup
Chillies (thinly sliced)	3
Fresh basil (chopped)	3 tbsp
Fresh parsley	1/2 tsp
Lemon (juice)	2 tsp
Salt	1/4 tsp
Balsamic vinegar	1 tsp
Olive oil	3 tbsp
Diced tomato for garnish	1

Method:
1. Cook lentils.
2. Drain, rinse and place lentils in a bowl.
3. Combine lentils with all remaining ingredients (except tomato). Toss gently.
4. Place in refrigerator.
5. Stir occasionally while salad is chilling.
6. Add tomato as garnish and serve.

ETHIOPIAN COOKBOOK

Tomato and Cucumber Salad
Quia

Preparation Time: 15 minutes
Cooking Time: 0 minutes

Serving Size: 4

Ingredients:

Tomatoes (seeded, diced)	2 cups
Cucumbers (diced)	1 ½ cups
Sweet onion (diced)	1/4 cup
Green hot pepper (seeded, diced)	1
Lemon (juice)	4 tsp
Balsamic vinegar	2 tsp
Salt	1/4 tsp
Black pepper	1/4 tsp
Olive oil	2 tsp

Method:
1. Toss together all ingredients.
2. Sprinkle with olive oil.

Hot Cabbage Salad
Tikil Gomen

Preparation Time: 10 minutes
Cooking Time: 45 minutes

Serving Size: 4 to 6

Ingredients:

Olive oil	3-4 tbsp
Carrots (thinly sliced)	4
Onion (thinly sliced)	1
Salt	1 tsp
Black pepper	1/2 tsp
Cumin	1/2 tsp
Turmeric	1/4 tsp
Cabbage (shredded)	1/2 head
Potatoes (cut in 1 inch cubes)	5

Method:

1. Heat the olive over medium heat in a medium skillet.
2. Add the carrots and onion. Cook in the hot oil for 5 minutes.
3. Add the salt, pepper, cumin, turmeric and cabbage. Cook 15 to 20 minutes.
4. Stir in the potatoes. Cover and reduce heat to low. Cook 15 to 20 minutes, or until potatoes are soft.

Little Fried Snacks
Dabo Kolo

Preparation Time: 15 minutes
Cooking Time: 15 minutes

Serving Size: 6 to 8

Ingredients:

All purpose flour	2 cups
Salt	1/2 tsp
Sugar	2 tbsp
Cayenne pepper	1/2 tsp
Oil	1/4 cup
Water	

Method:
1. In a 1-quart bowl mix flour, salt, sugar, cayenne pepper and oil.
2. Knead together and add water spoonful by spoonful to form stiff dough.
3. Knead dough for 5 more minutes.
4. Tear off a piece the size of a golf ball.
5. Roll it out with palms of hands on a lightly floured board into a long strip 1/2 inch thick.
6. Snip into 1/2 inch pieces with scissors.
7. Spread about a handful of the pieces on an ungreased 9 inch frying pan. Cook over heat until uniformly light brown on all sides, stirring up once in a while as you go along.
8. Continue until all are light brown. Serve as a snack.

ETHIOPIAN COOKBOOK

Fresh Cheese
Iab

Description: *Iab* is a fresh cheese similar to cottage cheese. Its cooling flavour is the perfect addition for many spicy Ethiopian dishes. *Iab* is often served as the finish to an Ethiopian meal.

Preparation Time: 3 minutes
Cooking Time: 0 minutes

Serving Size: 2 cups

Ingredients:

Cottage cheese	2 cups
Plain yogurt	1/2 cup
Lemon juice	2 tbsp
Salt	to taste
Black pepper	to taste

Method:
1. Place the cottage cheese, yogurt, lemon juice, salt and pepper into a large bowl and use a wooden spoon to stir together. Lightly mash the cheese curds.
2. Adjust seasoning and serve as a side dish or as the final course to an Ethiopian meal.

For Variation:
1. To make *Iab be Gomen* (Fresh Cheese with greens); stir in 2 cups of chopped and sautéed collard greens.
2. For added flavour, you can stir in chopped parsley, spinach or fenugreek leaves.
3. Fresh lemon zest can also be added.

Flaxseed Beverage
Telba

Description: *Telba* is a healthy and refreshingly creamy beverage.

Preparation Time: 25 minutes
Cooking Time: 5 minutes

Serving Size: 4 to 6

Ingredients:

Flaxseed	1 cup
Water	6 cups
Honey	2 tbsp

Method:
1. Heat a cast-iron skillet over low heat.
2. Add the flaxseed and dry roast it in the skillet, stirring for 5 to 10 minutes. Remove from heat and set aside to cool.
3. Place the toasted flaxseed in a spice grinder and grind to a powder. Sift through a medium-mesh sieve into a bowl.
4. Add the water to the flaxseed, stir and let set for 15 minutes to allow solids to settle out.
5. Strain to a pitcher. Add honey and chill before serving.

Honey Wine
Tej

Description: *Tej* is an Ethiopian sweet wine, similar to mead that is made from fermented honey. It is traditionally served from a vase-like vessel called a *berele*. This recipe is a rough approximation. Ethiopians believe *Tej* was the wine used for a toast between the Queen of Sheba and King Solomon.

Preparation Time: 5 minutes
Cooking Time: 10 minutes

Serving Size: 4 to 6

Ingredients:
Water	2 cups
Honey	1/3 cup
White wine (light, sweet white wine)	3 cups

Method:
1. In a small saucepan, heat the water and honey over low heat, stirring until the honey is completely dissolved.
2. Remove from heat and chill completely.
3. Pour the honey water and wine together into a decorative glass decanter, mix together and serve lightly chilled.

This book was written by Rachel Pambrun and Linda Johnson

in loving memory of Tatiana Titova-Smith,

and is dedicated to our beautiful granddaughter Mitike.

Made in the USA
Charleston, SC
10 September 2012